Whisky Traveler Great Britain

Whisky bars in England, Northern Ireland, Republic of Ireland, Scotland & Wales.

by
Paul Bissett

2022 edition

For all the hard-working whisky makers
across Great Britain.

Contents

Introduction

I like to travel, and I like to drink whisk(e)y, so I have been compiling a list of whisky bars for the last twelve years. Initially, just Scotch whisky, but it has expanded to cover all whiskies from bourbon, rye, Australian, Irish, Japanese, Canadian, scotch, Taiwanese, or any other type of whisk(e)y.

This book is the result of all the research that I put into ensuring that wherever I was headed to or hoped to go, I knew where I could find a "whisky bar" or a bar that sold whisky. What's the difference?

I believe that most people would recognize a "whisky bar," as a bar with hundreds of whiskies, whereas a bar that sells whiskies, in my mind would be a bar that at least sells a decent selection of whiskies, so not a "whisky bar" per se, but a darn sight better than a lot of bars, that seem hard pressed to offer two or three low end whiskies.
Another advantage to this book is that most of the bars listed also do good food, and many are good hotels. I have in the past booked a hotel for a trip because I knew it had a very good whisky bar.

I have not been disappointed in either the food or the accommodations associated with a good whisky bar on my travels.

That's the inspiration for this book; an on-hand guide for reading in advance of your trip, reading on the plane, or when you get to your hotel. You'll always find the closest whisky bar, or at least a bar with a good selection of whisky. Or just keep a copy on your bar as a conversation piece for you and your friends to compare notes on the whisky bars that you have been to.

I have tried for dedicated whisky bars where possible, but some cities just do not have any. So, you may find referenced; chain bars/hotels, Irish bars, Scottish bars, etc., but they will have the best whisky selections that I could find locally.
As we used to say in the Navy, "any port in a storm."

Finally, if you find a great whisky bar that is not listed in this book, email me (my email is on the last page of this book) the details and I will put it in the next edition with "*as recommended by ..... (your name), ... (city)."

England

Alnwick

- **The John Bull.** With over 120 different single malt whiskies.
  www.facebook.com/JohnBullAlnwick
  12 Howick Street.
  *As recommended by Stephen Wanless of Durham, England.

Birmingham

- **Grain & Glass.** With a nice whisky list of over 300 bottles.
  https://grainandglass.co
  75-80 Vyse Street, Hockley.

- **The Victoria.** With over 50 whiskies on offer.
  www.thevictoriabirmingham.co.uk
  48 John Bright Street.

Brighton

- **The Lion and Lobster.** Over 20 different whiskies.
www.thelionandlobster.co.uk
24 Sillwood Street.

Bristol

- **The Rummer**. Has close to 100 bottles of whisky from around the world.
www.therummer.net
All Saints Lane.

- **The Woods**. Good selection of single malt scotch with around 50 bottles at any given time.
www.facebook.com/TheWoodsBristol
1 Park Street Avenue.

Coventry

- **The Kenilworth**. Great cocktail bar with over 50 whiskies available.
www.thekenilworth.co.uk
61 Warwick Road.

Devon

- **The NoBody Inn.** With over 250 whiskies available.
  www.nobodyinn.co.uk
  Doddiscombsleigh, Near Exeter.
  *As recommended by Paul Munro of Exmouth, Devon.

Leeds

- **51% Bourbon Lounge.**   Home to one of the largest collections of bourbon in the UK and uses it in fantastic cocktails.
  www.facebook.com/51percentbourbon
  11-13 Hirst's Yard.

Liverpool

- **Bar Four.** The Hard Day's Night Hotel is a stylish tribute to the Fab Four. If you are a Beatles fan, you won't mind that there are only around 25 whiskies.
  www.harddaysnighthotel.com
  North John Street.

- **Mackenzie's Whisky Bar**. With a global selection of whiskies.
  www.mackenziesbar.co.uk
  32 Rodney Street.

London

- **American Bar at the Savoy Hotel, The Strand**. The American Bar at London's famed Savoy hotel took home three significant prizes at the "Spirited Awards, including the Award's most prestigious one: "World's Best Bar." The other two honors it took home are "Best International Bar Team" and "Best International Hotel Bar." It may not have a huge whisky list, but it does have whiskies and it's one helluva bar.
www.fairmont.com
The Strand.

- **Athenaeum, Mayfair**. Very nice whisky selection. This bar also does whisky and food pairings.
www.athenaeumhotel.com
116 Piccadilly, Mayfair.

- **Avenue Bar & Restaurant**. Over 50 whiskies available.
www.avenue-restaurant.co.uk
7-9 St James's Street.

- **Balls Brothers.** Small, but nice selection of whiskies.
www.ballsbrothers.co.uk/locations/austin-friars
10-11 Austin Friars.

- **Black Rock Tavern.** With over 250 whiskies from around the world.
  http://blackrock.bar
  9 Christopher Street.

- **Boisedale of Canary Wharf**. The bar, in the restaurant on the 2nd floor - a 12-metre-long glowing amber wall of liquid gold - holds over 1,000 bottles of single malt scotch whisky and is undoubtedly be one of the most extensive and magnificent whisky bars in the world.
  www.boisdale.co.uk
  Cabot Place, canary wharf.

- **Boisdale of Belgravia.** Sister establishment to the above bar and Restaurant.
  www.boisdale.co.uk
  15 Eccleston Street, Belgravia.

- **Boisdale of Bishopsgate.** Sister establishment to the above bars and Restaurants.
  www.boisdale.co.uk
  Swedeland Court, 202 Bishopsgate.

- **Boisdale of Mayfair.** Sister establishment to the above bars and Restaurants.
  www.boisdale.co.uk
  12 North Row, Mayfair.

- **Britannia Bar Smok'd.** BBQ food at its best
  and with a large whisky selection including
  American, English, Irish, Japanese, Scotch
  and Welsh.
  www.britannia.smokd.co.uk
  44 Kipling Street, Kipling Estate.

- **Bull in a China Shop.** With over a hundred
  whiskies.
  www.bullinachinashop.london
  196 High Street, Shoreditch.

- **Connought Hotel, Mayfair**. Not the largest
  of whisky lists, but there are some stellar
  whiskies listed. The Connaught Bar with its
  dusky pink Cubist decor, exclusive vintages
  and a stellar cocktail menu, the Connaught
  bar can be found at it its namesake hotel
  named 'The Best Bar in Europe' in The
  World's 50 Best Bars 2019.
  www.the-connaught.co.uk
  Carlos place, Mayfair.

- **Hide Below.** Basement Whisky bar with
  whiskies from around the world and over 100
  scotches. Hidden below "Hide" restaurant.
  www.hide.co.uk
  85 Piccadilly, Mayfair.

- **Merchant House.** With over 600 whiskies,
  400 Rums and 400 Gins.
  http://merchanthouse.bar
  13 Well Court, Off Bow Lane.

- **Nightjar**. Not the largest whisky list, but over 40 available. 'Think sharply attired staff, and top-notch drinks served in vintage Stemware.' Don't miss intriguing cocktail recipes revived from the 18th-century and Prohibition era.
  www.barnightjar.com
  129 City Road, Shoreditch.

- **Swift.** With over 300 whiskies to tempt your palate.
  www.barswift.com
  12 Old Compton Street, Soho.

- **Salt Whisky Bar.** Seymour Street. With over 180 whiskies (the bulk of which are single malt scotch whiskies) and Bourbons in stock.
  www.saltbar.com
  82 Seymour Street, Marble Arch.

- **The Bar at the Goring**. Small list of around 40 whiskies. Just a stone's throw from Buckingham Palace, luxury abounds at this exceptionally beautiful old-world bar.
  www.thegoring.com
  15 Beeston Place.

- **The Four Quarters**. With over 50 whiskies available, but you may not get peace to sip your dram as this is a retro arcade bar, think PacMan etc.
  https://fourquarters.bar
  Queen Elizabeth Olympic Park, 8, Canalside, E Bay Lane, Hackney Wick.

- **The Four Quarters**. With over 50 whiskies available, but you may not get peace to sip your dram as this is a retro arcade bar, think PacMan etc.
  http://geocities.fourquartersbar.co.uk
  187 Rye Lane, Peckham.

- **The Luggage Room**. With enough whiskies to sink a small boat. Advisable to book first as this is a small bar. Knock and enter.
  https://luggageroom.co.uk
  London Marriott Hotel, Grosvenor Square.

- **The Melody Whisky Bar at the St. Paul's Hotel**. With over 200 whiskies to try.
  www.melodywhiskybar.uk
  153 Hammersmith Road, Hammersmith.

- **The Sun Tavern**. With around 70 whiskies with an emphasis on Irish whiskey. They have a DJ playing most nights, so don't expect peace and quiet to sip your dram.
  www.thesuntavern.co.uk
  441 Bethnal Green Road.

- **The Vault at Soho**. With over 400 whiskies from around the world.
  www.thevaultsoho.co.uk
  3 Greek Street, Soho.

Manchester

- **Lost in Tokyo.** With around 30 different Japanese whiskies on offer.
  http://lostintokyo.co.uk
  26b Lever Street.

- **The Whisky Jar.** With over 300 whiskies on offer, from all over the world.
  www.thewhiskeyjar.com
  14 Tariff Street.

Ramsbottom

- **The Fisherman's Retreat.** With hundreds of whiskies.
  www.fishermansretreat.com
  Riding Head lane, Shuttleworth.
  *As recommended by Ian Thomas from Bolton, England.

Northern Ireland

Bangor

- **Fealtys.** With over 100 whiskies from around the world.
  www.facebook.com/fealtys-bangor-103229980339
  35 High Street.

Belfast

- **Bittles Bar.** Large selection of whiskies.
  www.facebook.com/BittlesBar
  70 Upper Church Lane.

- **Pug Uglys.** A large selection of whiskies, around 50 bottles, including Irish, Scotch and American.
  https://puguglys.com
  70 Upper Church Lane.

- **Henry's Bar.** Large selection of whiskies.
  www.henrysbelfast.com
  4 Joy's Entry.

- **McHugh's Bar.** Excellent selection of Irish Whiskey.
  www.mchughsbar.com
  29-31 Queen's Square.

- **Robinsons Bars.** 5 venues under one roof. If you're looking for whisky, head to the lounge which has a large selection of whiskies, including rare Irish and Scotch.
  https://robinsonsbar.co.uk
  38-40 Great Victoria Street.

- **Santeria.** An impressive whiskey list including Irish (of course) and Bourbon.
  www.santeriabelfast.com
  19 Fountain Street.

- **The "Cloth Ear" Bar at the Merchant Hotel.** An enormous spirit list, with tasting sessions of exotic premium spirits.
  www.themerchanthotel.com
  16 Skipper Street.

- **The Duke of York.** With the best selection of Irish whiskies in town (and they have Scotch as well).
  https://dukeofyorkbelfast.com
  Hill Street and Commercial Court.

- **The Errigle Inn.** With a nice selection of Irish, Scotch and American whiskies.
  https://errigle.com
  312-320 Ormeau Road.

- **The Jeggy Nettle.** With a good selection of whiskies.
  https://thejeggynettle.com
  12 Stranmillis Road.

- **The Linen Bar.** Nice selection of whiskies.
  www.tensquare.co.uk/Bar-Dining/Linen-Bar
  10 Donegall Square South.

- **The Morning Star.** With over 30 whiskies.
  www.themorningstarbar.co.uk
  7-19 Pottingers Entry.

- **The National & Sixty6 Bar.** With over 50 whiskies (Irish, Scotch, American, Japanese and Canadian).
  www.thenationalbelfast.com
  62-68 High Street.

- **The Points Whiskey & Alehouse.** With a large selection of whiskies. They also do whiskey tastings.
  www.thepointsbelfast.com
  44 Dublin Road.

- **White's Tavern.** Belfast's oldest tavern est. 1630. With a great selection of whiskies.
  www.whitestavernbelfast.com
  2-4 Winecellar Entry.

Bushmills

- **The Bushmills Inn.** With an extensive whiskey list.
  www.bushmillsinn.com
  9 Dunluce Road.

Enniskillen

- **Blakes of the Hollow.** Lots of premium of whiskies.
  http://blakesofthehollow.com
  6 Church Street.

Hillsborough

- **The Hillside.** Est. 1752. With an extensive selection of Gins and whiskies.
  www.hillsidehillsborough.co.uk
  21 Main Street.

- **The Vintage Rooms at the Plough Inn.**
  With an extensive selection of Irish whisky.
  http://ploughgroup.com/ploughinn
  3 the Square.

Lurgan

- **The Corner House.** With a fine selection of Irish whisky.
  www.cornerhousebar.com
  1 Derrymacash Road.

Magherafelt

- **Mary's Bar.** With a generous selection of Irish whisky.
  http://marys-bar.com
  10 Market Street.

Omagh

- **Bertha's Bar at the Silver Birch Hotel.** A good selection of whiskies.
  www.silverbirchhotel.com
  5 Gortin Road.

- **Bogan's Bar.** Nice selection of whiskies.
  www.facebook.com/bogansomagh
  26 Market Street.

Portadown

- **McConvilles.** A large selection of whiskies.
  https://whiskeyclub.com/bars/mcconvilles
  1 Mandeville Street.

Republic of Ireland

Ballyvaughan

- **O'Lochlainn's Whisky Bar.** With over 300 whiskies on offer.
www.facebook.com/OLochlainns-Bar-296085127145572
Ballyvaughan.

Bray

- **Harbour Bar.** With over 30 whiskies including Irish (of course), Scotch and Bourbons.
https://theharbourbar.ie
1-4 Dock Terrace.

Cahir

- **Malone's Galtee Inn.** Nice selection of whiskies.
www.facebook.com/galteeinn
The Square.

Clifden

- **Lowrey's Irish Music and whiskey Bar.**
  With over 100 Irish, Scotch and World
  Whiskies.
  www.lowrysbar.ie
  Market Street.

Cooley

- **Martin's Pub & Cooley whisky Bar.**
  Dedicated to Cooley whiskey products,
  including Greenore, Tyrconnell, Connemara
  and Kilbeggan whiskeys.
  No website at this time.
  Dundalk Road, Castlecarragh, Dundalk.

Dingle

- **Dick Mack's.** Est. 1899. A superb choice of
  Irish as well as some impressive international
  names.
  www.dickmackspub.com
  Green Street.

Dublin

- **37 Dawson Street.** Tucked in the back of this cool bar, is an even cooler old school whisky bar.
https://37dawsonstreet.ie
37 Dawson Street.

- **Alex Cocktail Bar at the Alex Hotel.** With a quality selection of Irish whiskey.
www.thealexdublin.ie
41-47 Fenian Street.

- **Bailey.** With Irish and American whiskies.
http://baileybarcafe.com
Duke Street, Off Grafton Street.

- **Bowes Lounge.** It's a pub in Dublin, of course it has whiskey!
www.bowespub.com
31 Fleet street.

- **Brian Boru.** This bar can be found on the Irish whiskey trail.
www.thebrianboru.ie
5 Prospect Road. Glasnevin.

- **Dingle Whiskey Bar.** Good selection of Irish, Scottish and American whiskies.
www.thewhiskeytrail.ie/2017/07/12/dingle-whiskey-bar
45-47 Nassau Street.

- **Johnnie Fox's**. Over 50 whiskies available.
  www.johnniefoxs.com
  Glen Cullen, Dublin Mountains (about 15 miles from the city center).

- **O'Donoghue's Pub**. Good selection of whiskies available.
  www.odonoghues.ie
  15 Merrion Row.

- **Temple Bar Pub.** With one of the largest whiskey collections in Ireland.
  www.thetemplebarpub.com
  47/48 Temple Bar.

- **The Jasmin Bar at the Brooks hotel.** The Venue of choice for Ireland's Irish Whiskey Society meetings. Whiskey tastings available.
  www.brookshotel.ie/jasmine-bar-and-cafe-lounge.html
  62 Drury Street.

- **The Long Hall.** Est. 1766. With over 50 whiskies available.
  No website at this time.
  51 South Great George's Street.

- **The Palace Bar.** Of course, it has whiskey.
  www.thepalacebardublin.com
  21 Fleet Street.

Galway

- **1520 Bar.** One of the largest spirit collections in Galway (on the Irish whiskey trail).
  https://1520.ie
  14 Quay Street.

- **An Púcán** (On Pookawn). With over 200 whiskies available (on the Irish whiskey trail).
  https://anpucan.ie
  11 Forster Street.

- **Blake's Bar.** Actually, a Brasserie, with a good selection of whiskies (on the Irish whiskey trail).
  https://brasseriegalway.com
  25 Eglinton Street.

- **Freeneys Bar.** Good selection of whiskey, enough whiskies to be on the Irish whiskey trail.
  https://irishpubs.ie/pub/freeneys-bar-2
  High Street.

- **Garavan's Bar.** Good selection of whiskey with Irish (obviously), Scotch and Bourbons (and enough whiskies to be on the Irish whiskey trail).
  www.garavans.ie
  46 William Street.

- **Garvey's Bar.** With a great selection of Irish whiskey in fact enough whiskies to be on the Irish whiskey trail.
  No website at this time.
  Foster Street, Eyre Square.

- **McSwiggans.** Lots of whiskey and on the Irish whiskey trail.
  http://mcswiggans.ie/#./home
  3 Eyre Street.

- **O'Connell's Bar.** More than enough whiskey to keep you happy and on the Irish whiskey trail.
  http://oconnellsbargalway.com
  8 Eyre Square.

- **Sonny Molloys.** With 5 bars that are open until 2am, 7 nights a week and enough whiskies to be on the Irish whiskey trail.
  www.frontdoorpub.com/sonny-molloys
  8 Cross Street & High Street.

- **The Dáil Bar** (Dawl). An Irish whiskey trail bar.
  https://thedailbar.com
  42-44 Middle Street.

Killarney

- **Courtney's Pub.** Small, but good whiskey list.
  https://courtneysbar.com
  Plunkett Street.

Kilkenny

- **Dylan Whiskey Bar.** Has a whiskey library with almost 200 whiskies.
  www.thedylanwhiskybar.com
  5 John Street.

Offaly

- **Hugh Lynch's Bar.** With over 70 whiskies available.
  http://hughlynchs.com
  Kilbride Street.

Midleton

- **JJ Coppinger's.** With a good selection of whiskey.
  www.jjcoppingers.ie
  55 Main Street.

- **Michael Canty's Pub.** This pub is listed on the Irish whiskey trail.
  www.facebook.com/cantysconnollyst
  Conolly Street.

- **The Mad Monk Bar.** Small, but good whiskey selection.
  www.madmonk.ie
  Church Lane.

Scotland

Aberdeen

- **CASC.** Craft Beer and Whisky bar with over 500 whiskies and a walk-in humidor specializing in Cuban cigars.
www.cascnation.com
7 Stirling Street.

- **Macleod House & Lodge.** A luxurious bar, which offers 'an extensive selection of Scottish and international malt whiskies. With a range of 'rare and highly sought-after releases… alongside well-known favorites and traditional Scottish brands.
www.trumphotels.com/macleod-house
Menie Cresent, Balmedie.

- **McGinty's "Meal & Ale"**
Relatively new pub with traditional decor (and modern touches, lots of TVs) serving Scottish favourites and classic pub food. A good selection of cask ales, draught beers, wines and spirits, including over 100 whiskies.
www.mcgintysmealanale.co.uk
504 Union Street.

- **The Grill Bar**. The oldest bar in Aberdeen with its interior noted for special historical interest. They have a collection of almost 600 single malt scotch whiskies which won them the accolade of 'Whisky Bar of the Year 2008', with all the staff trained to the highest degree of knowledge.
  www.thegrillaberdeen.co.uk
  213 Union Street.
  *As recommended by Gordon Craig from Paisley, Scotland.

- **The Marcliffe Hotel & Spa.** With over 100 single malt whiskies available.
  www.marcliffe.com
  North Deeside Road, Pitfodels.

- **The Tippling House.** With a nice selection of single malt whiskies. With whisky tastings once a week and a monthly whisky club meeting.
  www.thetipplinghouse.com
  4 Belmont Street.

Aberlady

- **Ducks Inn.** A Scotch Malt Whisky Society (SMWS) partner bar, with a nice whisky list.
  www.ducks.co.uk
  38 High Street.

Aberlour

- **The Dowans Hotel.** The Still Bar has gained a reputation as One of the Great Whisky Bars of The World, as awarded by Whisky Magazine. With a selection of over 500 whiskies.
www.dowanshotel.com
Dowans Road.

- **The Mash Tun.** Home to a wide and varied selection of whiskies, both single malts and blends, predominately from Speyside but also incorporating distilleries from the rest of Scotland. Included in this selection is the exclusive Glenfarclas Family Cask Collection. The Family Casks are a unique collection of 44 single cask whiskies, with one for each consecutive year from 1952 to 1995. The collection is unique as there is no other known collection of rare and old whiskies that covers 44 consecutive years from the same distillery.
www.mashtun-aberlour.com
8 Broomfield Square.

- **The Station Hotel.** With a selection of over 500 whiskies.
www.stationhotelspeyside.com
51 New Street, Rothes.

Applecross

- **Applecross Inn.** Award winning Inn with around 60 whiskies and a number of Scottish Gins.
  www.applecrossinn.co.uk
  Applecross, Wester Ross

Auchterarder

- **Gleneagles Hotel "The Blue Bar."** A unique addition to the Dormy Restaurant, right on the 18th hole of The King's and The Queen's golf courses, The Blue Bar is an opulent showcase for the velvety-smooth Johnnie Walker Blue Label whisky. With leather sofas, luxurious throws, a large circular fire-pit and a wide selection of Cuban cigars.
  www.gleneagles.com
  Auchterarder.

- **Gleneagles Hotel "The Century Bar.** "An unrivalled selection of over 120 single malt scotch whiskies.
  www.gleneagles.com
  Auchterarder.

Ballater (Royal Deeside).

- **The Deeside Inn's "Ceilidh bar.** Offering a variety of beers and wines and a wide range of single malt whiskies.
  www.crerarhotels.com
  13- 15 Victoria Road.

- **The Loch Kinord Hotel.** The bar is Listed as a single malt whisky embassy, not only for the nice selection of whiskies, but also for the whisky knowledge of the staff.
  www.lochkinord.com
  Ballater Road, Dinnet.

Bo'ness

- **Corbie Inn**. A real ale pub, with a good selection of single malt whiskies, and whisky tastings held in the bar.
  www.corbieinn.co.uk
  84 Corbiehall.

Brora

- **The Sutherland Inn.** Has a growing collection of over 220 single malt scotch whiskies and an impressive wine list to compliment the locally sourced and freshly prepared menu.
  www.sutherlandinn.co.uk
  Fountain Square.

Cabrach

- **The Grouse Inn**. The bar has to be seen to be believed and is one of the best-stocked Whisky Bars in Scotland with over 700 whiskies.
  www.dufftown.co.uk/prov_attr_detail.php?id=75
  Lower Cabrach.
  *As recommended by Rob Stables from Lumsden, Scotland.

Callendar

- **Poppies Hotel & Restaurant**. Cameron's bar has an extensive whisky list.
  www.poppieshotel.com
  Leny Road.

Campbeltown

- **Ardshiel Hotel**. Usquebaugh Bar and Lounge has a superb choice of over 700 whiskies. The staff are very friendly and knowledgeable. This bar is so good, I had many recommendations for it.
  www.ardshiel.co.uk
  Kilkerran Road.
  *As recommended by Jack Dunford of Laphroaig, Scotland.

Cove

- **Knockderry House Hotel.**   Another single malt whisky embassy.
www.knockderryhouse.co.uk
Shore road.

Craigellachie

- **Craigellachie Hotel**. This award-winning four-star hotel, two rosette restaurant and world-renowned Quaich Bar boasts 700 different Single Malt Scotch Whiskies.
http://craigellachiehotel.co.uk
Victoria Street.
*As Recommended by David McDonald of Magalia, California.

- **Highlander Inn**. The Highlander Inn is in the center of the village of Craigellachie, the heart of Scotland's Malt Whisky Trail. With an extensive collection of whiskies.
www.whiskyinn.com
Speyside way.
*As Recommended by Ivor Owens-Smith from Perth, Western Australia.

Dornoch

- **Dornoch Castle Hotel.** A great bar to go and sample single malts, with very knowledgeable staff.
www.dornochcastlehotel.com
Castle Street.

- **The Eagle Inn.** With a nice selection of whiskies and Gin.
http://eagledornoch.co.uk
Castle Street.
*As Recommended by Jim Smart from Dundee, Scotland.

Drumnadrochit

- **Benleva Hotel.** With its own brewery on site and a passion for whisky the Benleva is well worth a visit.
www.benleva.co.uk
Kilmore, Drumnadrochit.

- **Loch Ness Lodge Hotel**. The Pibroch whisky bar, carries a nice selection of single malt scotch whiskies. We stayed here when we hiked the Great Glen Way with friends.
www.lochness-hotel.com
Drumnadrochit.

- **Fiddler's Restaurant & Bar.** We ate and
  drank here both nights we spent in
  Drumnadrochit while hiking the Great Glen
  Way and availed ourselves of their Award-
  Winning Malt Whisky Bar, with over 400
  single malt scotch whiskies.
  www.fiddledrum.co.uk
  The Village Green.
  *As recommended by Dianne McKasson of
  Vacaville, California

Dufftown

- **Tannochbrae Hotel**. With over 300 whiskies
  available.
  www.tannochbrae.co.uk
  22 Fife Street.

Dundee

- **The Fort Hotel, Broughty Ferry**. Good
  whisky list. Winner 2008, 2009 and 2010
  of Dundee's Best Bar None award.
  www.fort-hotel.com
  48 - 60 Fort Street.

- **The Taybridge Bar**. Good whisky list of over
  100 whiskies.
  http://taybridgebar.co.uk
  129 Perth Road.

Easdale Island

- **The Puffer Bar.** With over 20 single malt whiskys including local Oban malts and many from Islay, and a nice selection of Scottish Gins.
http://pufferbarandrestaurant.co.uk
Easdale Island, Inner Hebrides.

Edinburgh

- **Abbotsford bar.** One of Edinburgh's finest traditional bars, with Rose Street's best selection of single Malt Scotch Whisky, so I had to try a few.
www.theabbotsford.com
3-5 Rose Street.

- **Albanach bar.** With over 250 single malt scotch whiskies on offer, well worth a visit if you are in the neighborhood.
www.belhavenpubs.co.uk/pubs/midlothian/albanach
197 High Street, Royal Mile
*As recommended by Ken Misch from Las Vegas, Nevada.

- **Amber Restaurant & Whisky Bar.** Award-winning food and over 440 whiskies. The restaurant, which is part of the Scotch Whisky Experience, offers whisky and food pairings.
www.scotchwhiskyexperience.co.uk
354 Castle Hill.

- **Angels Share hotel.** With a Good whisky list. My wife and I stayed here on a recent visit to Edinburgh and I even got a free whisky!
www.angelssharehotel.com
9 -11 Hope Street.

- **Arcade Haggis and Whisky Bar.** With an extensive whisky list.
www.facebook.com/thebesthaggis
48 Cockburn Street.

- **Balmoral Hotel**. "Scotch" is The Balmoral's new signature whisky bar offering over 500 whiskies in a variety of blends, malts and vintages dating back to 1940. I tried the Macallan 'M' here, quite expensive for a dram, but so worth it!
www.roccofortehotels.com/hotels-and-resorts/the-balmoral-hotel
1 Princes Street.

- **Bennet's Bar.** Is well known for its huge range of single malt scotch whiskies.
https://kilderkingroup.co.uk
8 Leven Street.

- **Black Cat.** With a nice selection of whiskies and an Ardbeg embassy as well.
www.facebook.com/theblackcatbaredinburgh
168 Rose Street.

- **Bon Vivant.** With a good number of whiskies available.
  www.bonvivantedinburgh.co.uk
  55 Thistle Street.

- **Bow Bar.** A traditional bar that offers more than 150 whiskies.
  www.thebowbar.co.uk
  On Victoria Street (also known as West Bow Street).

- **Bramble.** Cocktail bar with a large selection of whiskies.
  www.bramblebar.co.uk
  16a Queens Street.

- **Canny Mans**. 'No mobiles, no credit cards, no backpackers, no cameras' commands a sign in this unusual watering hole. The landlord can afford to be demanding, because this well-loved establishment is 'the best place in Morningside, if not in Edinburgh, for single malt scotch whisky, wines and cocktails'.
  www.cannymans.co.uk
  237 Morningside Road.

- **Dirty Dick's**. Pub at the West end of Rose Street, with over 200 malts to choose from.
  www.facebook.com/dirtydicksedinburgh
  159 Rose Street.

- **Element.** A collection of some of the finest Scottish malts from across the country, including everything from an 18-year-old Highland Park to a more baby-faced Macallan Gold.
  www.elementedinburgh.co.uk
  110-114 Rose Street.

- **George IV Bar**. With over 100 Single Malt Scotch Whiskies.
  www.georgeivbar.com
  54 George IV Bridge.

- **Guildford Arms**.   With a fine range of Single Malt Scotch Whiskies.
  www.guildfordarms.com
  1 West Register Street.

- **Jolly Judge.** Not a huge whisky selection, but it is a nice selection.
  www.jollyjudge.co.uk
  7 James Court (off the Royal Mile).
  *As recommended by Scott Chilvers of Newcastle upon Tyne, England.

- **Kay's Bar**. With a fine range of Single Malt Scotch Whiskies.
  www.kaysbar.co.uk
  39 Jamaica Street.

- **Kilderkin**. With a fine range of Single Malt Scotch Whiskies and regular whisky tastings.
  https://kilderkingroup.co.uk
  65 Canongate.

- **Leslies Bar.** Has over 60 single malt scotch Whiskies, which include Cask Bottling's and some Rare Expressions.
  No Website at this time.
  45-47 Ratcliffe Terrace.

- **Mitre.** With over 40 whiskies available.
  www.nicholsonspubs.co.uk
  131-133 High Street.
  *As recommended by Stuart Watkins of Edinburgh, Scotland.

- **Nauticus.** New whisky bar in Leith.
  nauticusbar.co.uk
  142 Duke Street.

- **Stockbridge Tap**. The bars whisky collection stretches to over a hundred single malt scotches, and a selection of blended whiskies and a diverse variety of bourbons.
  www.facebook.com/thestockbridgetap
  2-6 Raeburn Place.

- **Teuchters Bar.** The bar has over 100 Whiskies.
  http://teuchtersbar.co.uk
  26 William Street.

- **Teuchters Landing.** The bar has over 100 Whiskies.
  http://teuchtersbar.co.uk
  1a & 1c dock place.
  *As recommended by Danny Melville of Edinburgh, Scotland.

- **The Abbey Bar.** With a selection of over 120 whiskies available.
  http://abbeybar.co.uk
  65 S Clerk Street, Newington.

- **The Athletic Arms.** With a selection of over 250 whiskies available.
  www.facebook.com/DiggersEdinburgh
  1-3 Angle Park Terrace.

- **The Devil's Advocate.** Hundreds of whiskies available.
  https://devilsadvocateedinburgh.co.uk
  9 Advocate's Close.

- **The Dining Room & The Kaleidoscope Bar.** Residing within the walls of the much-revered Scotch Malt Whisky Society (SMWS). An ideal spot for either lunch or dinner (they offer both services six days a week). The selection of the Scottish Malt Whisky here is second to none in the city.
  https://smws.com/venues/28-queen-street
  28 Queen Street.

- **The Fiddler's Arms.** With a large whisky selection
  www.thefiddlersarms.com
  9-11 Grassmarket.

- **The Queens Arms.** Gastropub with a nice selection of whiskies.
  www.queensarmsedinburgh.com
  49 Frederick Street.

- **The Last Word Saloon.** With an extensive range of whiskies.
  www.lastwordsaloon.com
  44 St Stephen Street, Stockbridge.

- **The Royal Mile Tavern.** With over 100 whiskies.
  www.royalmiletavern.com
  127 High Street.

- **The Vaults.** The original home of The Scotch Malt Whisky Society (SMWS).
  https://smws.com/venues/the-vaults
  87 Giles Street.

- **Thomson's bar.** Offers an extensive array of Single Malt Scotch Whiskies, Casks Ales and Fine Wines.
  www.thomsonsbaredinburgh.co.uk
  182-184 Morrison Street.

- **Tigerlillie**. Serious eye candy Cocktail bar also has a nice selection of whisky.
  www.tigerlilyedinburgh.co.uk
  125 George Street.

- **Uisgebeatha.** Whisky bar of the year 2018. With over 400 whiskies on offer. Run by some of the most knowledgeable whisky geeks the capital has to offer.
www.usquabae.co.uk
2-4 Hope Street.

- **Voodoo Rooms.** Very elegantly decorated with a large whisky selection.
www.thevoodoorooms.com
19a West Register Street.

- **Waldorf Astoria, The Caley Bar.** One of Scotland's finest whisky bars with over 250 "water of life" varieties.
https://waldorfastoria3.hilton.com
Princes Street.

- **Whiski Bar, High Street**. With over 300 single malt scotch whiskies (not counting blends and Liqueurs), well worth a visit. Live Scottish music 7 nights a week.
www.whiskibar.co.uk
119 High Street.

- **Whiski Rooms, on The Mound**. This restaurant & bar is the glamorous new sister venue to Whiski on the Royal Mile. With over 300 whiskies.
www.whiskirooms.co.uk
4-7 North Bank Street.
*As recommended by Stuart Watkins of Edinburgh, Scotland.

- **White Hart inn**. Good choice of whiskies, I had a nice Glenmorangie 25-year-old with lunch in here. The White Hart's bar has a rich history of famous patrons, including Robert Burns, and the famous 'grave robbers', Burke and Hare. The cellar is said to date (1128) back to the first Inn built on this site whilst the building above ground dates to 1740.
  www.belhavenpubs.co.uk
  32-34 Grassmarket.

Eaglesham

- **The Swan Inn.** A good range of whiskies on offer.
  https://theswaninneaglesham.com
  23 Polnoon Street.

Edzell

- **Glenesk Hotel.** A Scotch Malt Whisky Society (SMWS) partner bar, with a nice whisky list.
  http://gleneskhotel.com
  High Street.

Forres

- **Knockomie Hotel**. The Malt Library has over 80 single malt scotch whiskies and unique blends from all the whisky producing areas of Scotland.
  www.knockomie.co.uk
  Granton Road.

Fort Augustus

- **The "Inch" Inchnacardoch hotel**. The Whisky bar has around 30 Single Malt and single cask whiskies. We stayed here when we hiked the Great Glen Way.
  www.inchhotel.com
  Fort Augustus.

Fort William

- **Creag Mhor Lodge's bar.** Has a collection of over 340 single malt scotch whiskies.
  www.creagmhorlodge.com
  North Ballachulish.

- **The Grog & Gruel.** We ate and drank here, prior to hiking the Great Glen Way. The bar has a nice selection of over 100 whiskies.
  www.grogandgruel.co.uk
  66 High Street.

Fortrose

- **The Anderson**. Over 260 single malt scotch whiskies available.
  www.theanderson.co.uk
  Union Street.

Fraserburgh

- **Cheers Café Bar & Tavern**. Over 300 single malt scotch whiskies available, over 1000 spirits in total.
  www.facebook.com/CheersCafeBarTavern
  10 Broad Street.

Glasgow

- **Bar Gandolfi**. The attic Bar may look like a lofty wine bar, but don't be fooled - Single Malt Scotch whisky is the specialty.
  www.cafegandolfi.com
  64 Albion Street.

- **Ben Nevis.** One of the West End of Glasgow's best-kept secrets. Open in its present incarnation since 1999, great whisky and Guinness, and a truly welcoming atmosphere.
  www.thebennevisbar.com
  1197 Argyle Street.

- **Bon Accord pub.** Has a fabulous selection of single malt scotch whiskies, with over 400 available.
  www.bonaccordweb.co.uk
  153 North Street.

- **Carlton George Hotel.** 6 Unique bars covering 3 levels which are linked together by a maze of staircases and passageways. The Carlton George is an official single malt whisky embassy.
  www.carlton.nl/en/hotel-george-glasgow
  44 West George Street.

- **Corinthian bar and restaurant**. Over 40 whiskies, with an emphasis on Macallan flights.
  www.thecorinthianclub.co.uk
  191 Ingram Street.

- **Dram**. With an extensive whisky range.
  www.dramglasgow.co.uk
  232-246 Woodlands Road, Charing Cross.

- **Lismore**. The bar itself boasts a range of more than 150 Malt Whiskies, with a number of single-cask and independent bottlings. Traditionally on Tuesday and Thursday evenings the bar hosts Gaelic music sessions.
  No website at this time.
  206 Dumbarton Road.

- **MacSorley's**. With a nice whisky list and a haunt of the Glasgow whisky club.
  https://macsorleys.co.uk
  42 Jamaica Street.

- **Oran Mor pub**, (formerly Kelvinside Parish Church). The Whisky Bar at the Oran Mor is one of the west end's most popular destinations, boasting over 280 single malt scotch whiskies.
  www.oran-mor.co.uk
  Top of Byers Road.

- **Piper whisky bar.** Extensive whisky selection, including a whisky from every distillery in Scotland.
  www.thepiperbar.com
  57 Cochrane Street, George Square.
  *As Recommended by Bob Skinner & Molly Navarro-Skinner from Redding, California.

- **Pot Still.** With over 700 single malt scotch Whiskies. Popular with stars of stage and screen who frequent it.
  www.thepotstill.co.uk
  154 Hope Street.
  *As recommended by Harry Andrew of Glasgow, Scotland.

Glencoe

- **Clachaig Inn.** With over 365 whiskies available. This pub has been famous for centuries and is just what you need/want after a hard day in the hills. The atmosphere is fabulous with like-minded outdoors types from all over the world. We stayed here the last time we hiked the West Highland Way.
www.clachaig.com
Glencoe.

- **The Glencoe Hotel.** As a Scotch Whisky Embassy, the bar stocks a wide selection of single malt whiskies from around Scotland.
www.crerarhotels.com/the-glencoe-inn
Glencoe Village.

Grantown-on-Spey

- **The Craiglynne Hotel.** Offering a full range of single malts.
https://bespokehotels.com/craiglynne
Woodlands Terrace.

Helensburgh

- **The Clyde Bar.** The bar has a great selection of over 100 single malt scotch whiskies.
www.theclydebar.com
62-64 West Clyde Street.

Huntly

- **Castle Hotel, The Distillery bar.** With a selection of over 140 Single Malt scotch and Blended whiskies.
  www.castlehotel.uk.com
  Portsoy Road.

Inveraray

- **George Hotel.** With over 100 whiskies on offer.
  www.thegeorgehotel.co.uk
  Main Street East.
  *As recommended by Albert Calland of Wigan, England.

- **Loch Fyne Hotel & Spa.** With many single malts. Also, Glen Ord, Dalmore and Teaninich distilleries are less than a 30-minute drive from the hotel.
  www.crerarhotels.com
  Strathpeffer.

Invermoriston

- **The Glemoriston Arms.** The hotel bar has a nice stock of single malt scotch whisky and a nice outside area to sit in the evening and enjoy your single malt. We stayed here when we hiked the Great Glen Way.
www.glenmoristonarms.co.uk
Invermoriston.

Inverness

- **Culloden House Hotel.** The Restaurant & Bar brim with Malt Whiskies, recognized as a Malt Whisky Embassy by the Scottish Malt Whisky Society. With many malts that are rare and, exclusive. 160 of the best bottles around.
www.cullodenhouse.co.uk
Inverness.

- **The Malt Room.** With an extensive selection of over 200 single malts.
www.themaltroom.co.uk
34 Church Street.

- **The Palace Hotel**. The bar has a good stock of single malt scotch whisky and a nice view across the river to Inverness Castle. We stayed here when we hiked the Great Glen Way.
www.bw-invernesspalace.co.uk
8 Ness Walk.

Isle of Arran

- **Lochranza hotel.** With a whisky list that surpasses 500 bottles you're spoiled for choice.
www.lochranzahotel.co.uk
Lochranza.

Isle of Eriska

- **Isle of Eriska hotel.** Winner of "Great whisky bars of the world" gold award. An impressive collection of single malt scotch whiskies.
www.eriska-hotel.co.uk
Benderloch.

Isle of Islay

- **Ballygrant Inn & Restaurant**. Robolls bar has a nice stock of over 400 whiskies.
www.ballygrant-inn.com
Ballygrant.

- **Bowmore hotel.** With over 700 whiskies available.
https://bowmorehotel.co.uk
Jaimeson Street, Bowmore.
*As recommended by Jack Dunford of Laphroaig, Scotland.

- **Bridgend Hotel.** A well-stocked bar with a variety of famous Islay malts plus a selection of local ales.
  http://bridgend-hotel.com
  Bridgend.
  *As recommended by Dan Reid of Citrus Heights, California.

- **Harbour Inn**. The Schooner bar has all the Islay single malt whiskies, as well as many from the other whisky regions.
  www.bowmore.com/harbour-inn
  The Square, Bowmore.

- **Islay house.** A Scotch Malt Whisky Society (SMWS) partner bar, with a nice whisky list.
  www.islayhouse.co.uk
  Bridgend.

- **Lochside Hotel.** The bar has a good selection of over 300 whiskies.
  www.lochsidehotel.co.uk
  20 Shore Street, Bowmore.
  *As recommended by Jack Dunford of Laphroaig, Scotland.

- **Port Askaig hotel.** With a nice selection of whiskies.
  www.portaskaig.co.uk
  Port Askaig.

- **Port Charlotte hotel.** Pride of place in the rounded central bar at this friendly hotel goes to an exceptional collection of about 140 Islay and rare Islay single malt scotch whiskies.
www.portcharlottehotel.co.uk
Port Charlotte.
*As recommended by David McDonald of Magalia, California.

- **The Machrie Hotel and Golf Links.** With a nice selection of whiskies.
www.campbellgrayhotels.com/machrie-islay-scotland
Port Ellen.

Isle of Jura

- **The Jura Hotel.** Located a few yards from the Jura Distillery. With an exclusive in-house Jura whisky that is not available anywhere else in the world.
www.jurahotel.co.uk
Craighouse.

Isle of Mull

- **Isle of Mull Hotel & Spa**. The Muileach bar has a good collection of over 100 drams just begging to be tasted.
www.crerarhotels.com/isle-of-mull-hotel-spa
Craignure.

- **Macgochans**. With a collection of over 100 whiskies available.

Kenmore (Perthshire)

- **The Kenmore hotel**. The Poets Bar offers a wide variety of fine Scottish malt whiskies.
www.kenmorehotel.com
The Square.

Loch Lomond

- **The Ardlui hotel.** Is listed as a whisky ambassador, so as you would expect. It has a well-stocked bar with a good selection of single malt scotch whisky.
I stayed here the first time I hiked the West Highland Way.
www.ardlui.com
Ardlui.

- **The Inn on Loch Lomond.** Enjoy a selection of 250 whiskies. Scottish hospitality continues at the weekends with traditional live folk music. We stayed here on a recent visit to Scotland.
www.innonlochlomond.co.uk
Luss.

- **The Oak Tree Inn.** The bar has a selection of over 50 single malt scotch whiskies. We stayed here the last time we hiked the West Highland Way.
  www.theoaktreeinn.co.uk
  Balmaha.

- **The Rowardennan Hotel.** Choose between the Rob Roy and Clansman bars, for a nice selection of single malt whisky. We stayed here the last time we hiked the West Highland Way.
  www.rowardennanhotel.co.uk
  Rowardennan.

Nairn

- **Golf view hotel & Spa**. Guests at the hotel bar are encouraged to sample some of the many, fine single malt whiskies on offer.
  www.crerarhotels.com/golf-view-hotel-spa
  63 Seabank Road.

Oban

- **Cuan Mor Restaurant and bar**. Go through the back of the building and you will find the Oban Bay Micro Brewery and a huge selection of single malts, the most exclusive of which you will find behind a locked iron cage.
  www.cuanmor.co.uk
  60 George Street.

Old Meldrum

- **Meldrum House Hotel.** The cave Bar has around 120 whiskies including one of the largest collections of Glen Garioch whiskies.
  www.meldrumhouse.com
  Old Meldrum.

Orkney

- **Orkney Hotel.** With over 1,000 whiskies on offer, you should probably book into the hotel for the night (or longer).
  www.orkneyhotel.co.uk
  40-41 Victoria Street, Kirkwall.

Partick

- **Bag O' Nails.** With a large whisky list including scotch and whiskies from around the world.
  https://bag-o-nails.co.uk
  165 Dumbarton Road.

Perth

- **Dickens Malt House.** The bar has well over 100 single malt Scotch whiskies.
  www.dickensbar.co.uk
  On the corner of South Street and South Methven Street.

Pitlochry

- **Athol Palace Hotel**. The Stagshead Bar has a fine selection of single malt scotch whiskies. I know, we stayed there.
www.athollpalace.com
Pitlochry.

- **Fisher's Hotel**. Gladstone's Bar has a fine selection of single malt scotch whiskies.
www.fishershotelpitlochry.com
75-79 Atholl Road.

- **Scotland's Hotel and Leisure Club.** With a collection of over 40 Scottish single malt whiskies to choose from.
https://scotlandshotel.com
40 Bonnethill Road.

- **The Old Mill.** With a nice collection of single malt whiskies to choose from.
www.theoldmillpitlochry.co.uk
Mill Lane.

Scourie

- **Edrachilles Hotel**. This is an accredited Scotch Whisky Embassy with its own qualified Whisky Ambassador and over 100 single malt scotch whiskies in stock.
www.eddrachilles.com
A894 2 miles South of Scourie.

Shetland

- **Busta House Hotel**. With a selection of around 225 single malt whiskies.
  www.bustahouse.com
  Busta.

Skye

- **Kinloch Lodge.** Not the biggest selection of single malts, but some really nice and hard to come by ones. David McDonald and I had a 42-year-old Macallan with dinner, which was quite superb. They also have a wonderful restaurant.
  https://kinloch-lodge.co.uk
  Sleat.
  *As recommended by David McDonald of Magalia, California.

- **Skeabost Country House.** The bar is well stocked with a wide selection of malt whiskies.
  www.skeabosthotel.com
  Skeabost Bridge.

- **Sligachan Hotel.** Found right in the heart of the Cuillin mountains, this bar is a favourite among climbers who like a wee dram after a hard day's scramble. The old-fashioned pine-clad bar may not win design awards, but its contents (namely 400 different varieties of single malt whiskies) make for an impressive choice of beverage.
  www.sligachan.co.uk
  Sligachan.

- **The Cuillin Hills Hotel.** Restaurant & Bar have their own dedicated Malt Bar called the Malt Embassy where you can relax and enjoy from over 130 malt whiskies.
  www.cuillinhills-hotel-skye.co.uk
  Portree.

- **The Stein Inn, Hotel, Restaurant & Bar.** A fine selection of 130 Malt Scotch whiskies.
  https://thesteininn.co.uk
  Waternish.

St. Andrews

- **The Keys Bar**. With over 300 whiskies available.
  No website at this time.
  87 Market Street.

- **The Old Course Hotel**. The Road Hole Bar, on the merit of this iconic bar, the Old Course Hotel achieved Whisky Hotel of the World Supreme status in the 2008 'Icons of Whisky' awards by Whisky Magazine, placing it within the top 25 per cent of the world's best whisky bars and restaurants.
  www.oldcoursehotel.co.uk
  Old Station Road.

- **The Old Manor Hotel**. A single malt whisky embassy.
  www.theoldmanorhotel.co.uk
  55 Leven Road.

Stirling

- **The Curly Coo Bar**. Specializing in Malt Whiskies, with a growing selection from across the regions of Scotland, and over 130 to choose from.
  www.curlycoobar.com
  51 Barnton Street.

Strathkinness

- **Strathkinness Tavern.** Located about 10 miles west of the town of St. Andrews and has around 70 whiskies on offer.
  www.strathkinnesstavern.co.uk
  4 High Road.

Strathpeffer

- **Ben Wyvis Hotel**. Sample an extensive range of over 60 whiskies. Also, Glen Ord, Dalmore and Teaninich distilleries are less than a 30-minute drive away.
  https://strathmorehotels-thebenwyvis.com
  Strathpeffer.

Tarbert

- **Stonefield Castle**. A single malt whisky embassy.
  www.bespokehotels.com
  Loch Fyne.

Troon

- **The Piersland House Hotel**. This hotel is an official single malt scotch whisky embassy.
  www.piersland.co.uk
  Craigend Road.

Wester Ross

- **The Torridon Hotel.** Scottish Hotel of the year 2011. With over 365 single malt whiskies on its shelves, the Whisky & Gin Bar also offers 120 Gins.
  www.thetorridon.com
  By Achnasheen.

Wick

- **The Mackay Hotel, Restaurant & Bar.** With
165 Whiskies available.
www.mackayshotel.co.uk
Union Street.

Wishaw

- **Artisan Restaurant**. With over
1300 whiskies available.
http://artisan-restaurant.com
249-251 Main Street.

Wales

Cardiff

- **Barley and Rye.** Nice selection of whiskies.
  www.barleyandrye.co.uk
  2 Greyfriars Road.

- **Lab 22.** Cocktail bar with whiskies from around the world and whisky tastings.
  www.lab22cardiff.com
  22 Caroline Street.

- **The Dead Canary.** Cocktail Bar with a nice selection of whiskies.
  https://thedeadcanary.co.uk
  Barrack Lane, St Davids Centre.

Llangennith

- **Kings Head Inn.** With one of the largest single malt whisky collections outside of Scotland.
  https://kingsheadgower.co.uk
  Clos Street, Cenydd.

Bibliography

(With thanks to)

Facebook
No website at this time.

My friends
(For recommending great bars)

My mum and dad
(For my being born and raised in Scotland)

My wife Tracey
for suffering through my many expeditions to
find whisky bars.

The British Royal Navy
(For taking me drinking all over the world)
https://www.royalnavy.mod.uk

The Scotch Malt Whisky Society
www.smws.com

Trip Advisor
www.tripadvisor.com

Whisky Advocate Magazine
http://whiskyadvocate.com/magazine

Whiskey Club
https://whiskeyclub.com

Biography

Paul Bissett was born in Edinburgh, Scotland and raised in the village of Blackness on the river Forth. At the age of seventeen he embarked upon a twenty-three-year career in the British Royal Navy, which took him all over the world. He has lived and worked in seven different countries.

He has, at various times been; a mountain guide; made and installed kilns in Australia; an instructor in Saudi Arabia; a Documentation Manager for a software company in Taiwan; and in the USA been a salesman for Sears, a firefighter, an Emergency Medical Technician (EMT), a jewelry store manager, senior case manager for the National Expert Witness Network based in Paradise, California and recently became an Independent Contractor for International Network in Advance-Gaming Inc., covering California.

Outside of work, he conducts Celtic and Scottish weddings. Hosts whiskey tastings, in California, Nevada and Oregon.

For fun, he researches whisky bars, writes/edits a whisky newsletter that go out to readers in ten different countries.

He also gives talks on all things Scottish and has been the Master of Ceremonies at many events all over the world, including the Las Vegas Celtic Games (twice).

He currently lives in Yuba City, California, with his wife Tracey and their three dogs, Heather, Hamish and Luna.

Also, by Paul Bissett;

A Whisky Might Not Fix Things, But It's Worth A Shot! - Whisk(e)y related: Anecdotes, Humor, Jokes, Memes, Quotes, Toasts & Trivia.

Cigar Traveler - A guide to Cigar lounges in USA.

Destiny's Bite - A children's story (A follow up to Winter's Bite). A modern-day adventure set in Scotland and based on Scottish mythology.

From Milngavie to Midges - Hiking the "West Highland Way, Scotland."

Hiking with Nessie - Hiking the "Great Glen Way, Scotland."

Scotland's Single Malt Whisky Distilleries. Where they are, when they were founded, how to pronounce their names (and what those names mean). I have also included a review of a whisky from each distillery.

Touring Scotland - A guide to help you plan the trip of a lifetime

Whisky Timeline - Whisk(e)y distilleries around the world and when they were founded.

Whiskey Traveler - A guide to Whisk(e)y bars around the world.

Whiskey Traveler - America – Whiskey bars in every state.

Winter's Bite - A children's story. A modern-day adventure set in Scotland and based on Scottish mythology.

Available at www.amazon.com

My email is; paulwbissett@outlook.com

My website is; www.scot-talks.com